THE VALE OF TODMORDEN

Also by Herbert Lomas

Chimpanzees are Blameless Creatures (Mandarin Books, 1969)
Who Needs Money? (Blond & Briggs, 1972)
Private and Confidential (London Magazine Editions, 1974)
Public Footpath (Anvil Press, 1981)
Fire in the Garden (OUP, 1984)
Letters in the Dark (OUP, 1986)
Trouble (Sinclair-Stevenson, 1992)
Selected Poems (Sinclair-Stevenson, 1995)
A Useless Passion (London Magazine Editions, 1999)

Translations from the Finnish

Territorial Song (London Magazine Editions, 1981)
Contemporary Finnish Poetry (Bloodaxe Books, 1991)
Wings of Hope and Daring Poems by Eira Stenberg (Bloodaxe Books, 1992)
Fugue Poems by Kai Nieminen (Musta Taide, Helsinki, 1992)
Black and Red Poems by Ilpo Tiihonen (Making Waves, 1993)
The Eyes of the Fingertips are Opening Poems by Leena Krohn (Musta Taide, Helsinki, 1993)
Narcissus in Winter Poems by Risto Ahti (Making Waves, 1994)
The Year of the Hare A novel by Arto Paasilinna (Peter Owen, 1995)
Two Sequences for Kuhmo Poems by Lauri Otonkoski (Kuhmon Kamarimusikin Kannatusyhdistys RY, 1994)
Eeva-Liisa Manner: Selected Poems (Making Waves, 1997)
Three Finnish Poets (London Magazine Editions, 1999)
A Tenant Here: Selected Poems of Pentti Holappa (The Dedalus Press, 1999)
Gaia: a Musical for Children, by Ilpo Tiihonen (Suomen Kansallisteatteri, 2001)
Not Before Sundown A novel by Johanna Sinisalo (Peter Owen, 2003)

The Vale of
Todmorden
HERBERT LOMAS

Arc Publications
2003

Published by Arc Publications
Nanholme Mill, Shaw Wood Road
Todmorden OL14 6DA, UK

Copyright © Herbert Lomas 2003

Design by Tony Ward
Printed by Antony Rowe Ltd.,
Eastbourne, E. Sussex

ISBN 1 900072 81 5

Earlier versions of about a quarter of the poems in this
book appeared in the sequence 'Todmorden' in
Public Footpath by Herbert Lomas (Anvil Press, 1981)

The author acknowledges his indebtedness to the
photographs in Roger Birch's
A Way of Life: Glimpses of Todmorden Past
(E. J. Morten, the Scolar Press Ltd, 1972)

Cover photograph by Tony Ward

The publishers acknowledge financial assistance
from the Arts Council of England, Yorkshire.

Editor, UK & Ireland: Jo Shapcott

The word of the Lord came unto me again, saying, What mean ye, that ye use this proverb concerning the land of Israel, saying, The fathers have eaten sour grapes, and the children's teeth are set on edge? As I live, saith the Lord God, ye shall not have occasion any more to use this proverb in Israel.

– Ezekiel, xviii 1-3

*When thee and me
Played in t' muck
We little knew
Our marvellous luck.*

– Ted Hughes

CONTENTS

Pennine Way / 9
The Black Swan / 10
Water / 11
Buckley Wood / 12
Grandfather Garner / 13
Granma Garner / 14
Millstone Grit / 16
In the Old Black Swan / 17
Swag / 18
Carter / 19
Miles Weatherill at the Vicarage / 20
Miles Weatherill at the Black Swan / 21
Freedom / 22
Performing for Granma Lomas / 23
Grandfather Lomas / 24
The Town Hall / 25
Princes and Toads / 26
Cornets and Trumpets / 27
Soldiers / 28
Dad / 29
Rochdale Road / 31
Mr Hyde / 33
Tram and Bert / 34
Brass / 35
Rebuilding / 36
The Rochdale Canal / 37
Fly / 39
Darkness / 40
Gulliver / 41
Chemistry / 42
Science / 43
Lifeboat Day / 44
Mad Mouse / 45

Keith / 46
Rabbit / 47
Kiss / 48
Dobroyd Castle / 49
Drink / 50
Love / 52
Billy Holt / 54
Fathers, Sons and Daughters / 55
Where Are You Now? / 57
Roomfield School / 58
Urine / 60
Books at School / 61
Our Headmistress / 62
All the Animals of Empire / 63
Knickers / 64
Teachers / 65
Aquariums / 66
Olga / 67
Marjorie Green / 68
Mary Priestley / 69
The Rechabite Concert Party / 71
Sin / 73
Stoodley Pike / 74
Listening / 75
Rupert / 76
Dog Show / 77
Albion Barker / 78
Gramophone / 79
Christ Church / 80
The Choirmaster / 81
Choirboys / 82
Seeing Stars / 83
Funeral March / 84

Ridge-Foot House / 85
Leaving the Choir / 86
Slump / 87
The Golden Lion / 88
Depression / 89
The Sentence / 90
Auntie Edith / 91
Uncle Herbert Rexstrew / 92
Tommy Dodd the Daisher / 93
Goodbye to the Vale / 95
Writer's Workshop at Lumb Bank / 96
Cross Stone Church / 97
Haworth / 98
'Artemidorus Farewell' / 99

Biographical Note / 101

PENNINE WAY

    1.
We sailed from the North German Plain,
splashed down on East Anglia's coast,
plundered and murdered our way
north-west over England to the Pennines
and settled round the well in the little narrow cleft,
stealing our neighbours' sheep and horses
and listening to Beowulf in the evenings.
But after that, farmers, millworkers,
dyemasters, soldiers, survivors, sometimes
impregnated by randy gentry, we went
down in the world, and up, and down again,
till there were none of us in the valley,
though the valley was still in us.

    2.
This valley's beautiful not picturesque.
The folk who raised their heads to Stoodley Pike
had ears clubbed deaf by the ramming of looms.
The clog feet that clattered by the bedroom window
had squatted silently outside the peaceful mills
when humiliation threatened in the General Strike.
This is a cold country and a wet and the stones drizzle
on the moor sides and on the houses and on the tops.
The steep tilt of the valley drops the dark
fast in the evening: it's suddenly cold,
you're conscious of night. After the day's toil
toasted teacakes are buttered by the fire,
or water's hot in a tin bath with the flames on your skin.
The benighted streets are empty. The old houses
have black corners that seem occupied. Wind
buffets from Whirlaw to Stoodley, compelled by love
to the wisest and sometime cruellest thing
for the welfare of a people.

THE BLACK SWAN

Out of what black hole where my grandfather's standing
did I run as a boy? Behind whose parlour windows was I watching
the flies buzzing, tracing raindrop tracks, yearning?
Behind which bedroom window lay I in bed fearing
the damp-marks leering on the ceiling, hearing
the clogs of the millworkers in the morning,
imagining another track through buttercups, pollen and bees,
as I lay there with measles watched over by vampires?

It's a black swan that sailed past the black hole looking
towards my mother's and father's two windows
where they lay together suffering in their happier half-mad days.

And later came the demolitions and the rebuildings,
the end of the stained glass, the creaking landings,
the ruin of the eighteenth-century irrationality,
the night-kept rooms in the right tangle for the family,
bats sitting around in a circle waiting.

The demolitions first and then the breakdowns
in a house that still exists though not in stone.

WATER

I grip the mahogany
rim of the bath, try to
stand naked in the Pears-soap

lathering scent and the steam's
flat Pennine smell but need
my mother's hand to steady me.

At the paddling pool,
leaning down over the concrete
rim, I bend just too far,

tip over head down,
and I can't pull my head out
from under the water –

gulping, drowning, but Gladys
rushes over, pulls me out,
and it makes me dream

I'm smothering, being born.

BUCKLEY WOOD

Fingers trail and graze along a stone wall,
kissed by the scratch touch in the grit.

The soaking green-streaked beech trees
stretch their barks and grope for the sky.

Steep up, and puffing you out, Bluebell Wood
makes you wade knee-high through wet stalks.

You squeeze the stalks close to the bulb,
and they squeak and bleed stickily as they break.

A thick bunch is bouncing and rainy,
and their white stalks, glassed in a jar,

bring the hand-wetting drench and feel
of the long stems home to your house.

The sting of stone and bluebell skin
and the blue blur of the bells take your eyes

to the wet soil and another hot day too, when
a cloud of bees could set you running,

and they light up the bedroom where the dark's
full of holes going out and out and on and on forever.

GRANDFATHER GARNER

Grandfather Garner's dead, but he
and Granma still peep out of the sepia.

They're old twins but with completely
uncrinkly faces: little children

wrapped in yellowing flesh:
two faces with nothing to hide

and hiding nothing. His face is
my baby face at my christening

but wearing a beard and glasses.
But before his factory crashed

and he said to his Mason friends
Nay, Ah've lost me awn brass,

Ah'm noan losin nob'dy else's
did he sweat little kids like the others did?

GRANMA GARNER

Granma sits by the black-leaded fireplace
with its black kettle on the hob.

Her hair's split down the middle,
her glasses little golden ovals

with kind eyes watching her kitchen world.
Her memory's gone.

I'm eating mashed potatoes
and she says *Mind the bones*.

It makes me cross. I'm crawling
the kitchen carpet with a grumpy cat

who doesn't trust me,
and neither do I trust her.

We share the dark under the table
tipped by a bobble-fringed tablecloth.

I keep trying to stroke her fur
but have to keep pulling my hand back

from the sudden claws. Granma
smells old in her rustling satin,

but then I see her in her coffin
with the blond wood and silver handles,

where I've been told not to look.
Her nose is sharp and pointy above

white satin. It's the nose of Scott,
frozen, flat on his back in the ice,

and my nose tells me
there's another smell in the house.

MILLSTONE GRIT

Yes, there's the Pike, stiff black nipple
in the wind that strokes the sterile tops,
squeezing out stone for these cottages,
mills and churches, conducting blackness
into generations of sons that strut
the drystone walls with their teeth on edge.

Light can't nuzzle inside the cold cross
of Cross Stone Church but licks the four
black ears that tip the tower. The grit's
everywhere, in the cottage walls, in the bones
breaking out of the ruptured hillsides
with their crumble of afterbirth.

The hawthorns are prickly black,
the gravestones are black,
and as evening drops its cold
the moors go black, blackening the valleys.
Light breaks through the mourning,
the clouds crack and slant down light.

The wind jumps in your nostrils,
makes your lungs rear, and you know
you've got it, whatever it is, under your chest,
behind your brain and mind. The wind
is lice in your hair, saying what you
only hear on the moors and can't say.

IN THE OLD BLACK SWAN

Everything has always been
just like this: the bobbled tablecloth,

the prickly black chaise-longue,
the rain, the cotton mills,

the canal with its tadpoles,
sticklebacks and water-beetles,

the stone towpath, the black hawthorns,
and the early-morning clogs under my window.

They've always clacked by in the dark
at six o'clock every day. It's always been like this.

I'm on the sideboard, drumming dents
with my heels, then I crawl the floor

with my cattle and sheep, walk the lead dog
over the fields to my farm,

raise and lower the drawbridge on my fort.
I'm the besieger and the besieged.

SWAG

Among the pearls, brooches, and oval gold cameo
on my mother's dressing table gleam five gold discs.

Suddenly my mother notices her gold sovereigns
are gone. But I know where they are, and I'll show her.

I take her to my secret hiding-place, under
the newspaper, in the cupboard, in Gladys's house.

Together we smell the raw wood and the paper
and stare at the cache of gleaming golden treasure.

CARTER

He heaves a great clog on a moving spoke,
lobs upwards as the cart moves forward,
vaults on the platform with clicking tongue
and jerks on the reins and stands up bouncing
as the big-wheeled iron-tyred cart and its load
bone-rattle over cobbles and down the road.

Who's this huge man, cords corded at the knee,
mastering this straining and steaming and stamping
in bright brass? Invisibly he dekkoes round
at the dripping cottages, the running-down mills
and the drystone walls, as he pulls the reins
of his drayhorses, shaking shaggy fetlocks

like girls' hair above the mud. Look in his eye
for more than a moment, and you see
the conquistador, the desperado, the brigand,
the Cossack, the lover, rapist and killer,
and you look down, as you must,
from what you daren't understand.

MILES WEATHERILL AT THE VICARAGE

Miles's secret meetings with his sweetheart,
seventeen-year-old Sarah Bell,
had been snitched on by Jane Smith.

So the Vicar and his wife
dismissed Sarah from their service.
Miles stopped at the Black Swan for a stiffening whisky

and then he was at the vicarage,
with four pistols and an axe,
savaging the Vicar and his wife.

He shot the children's nurse, Jane Smith,
then quietly awaited his arrest
and was hanged at New Bailey Prison.

It was Manchester's last public execution,
with more than a thousand people watching
while Miles Weatherill met his ill weather.

MILES WEATHERILL AT THE BLACK SWAN

One Wednesday night in the 1970s glasses
explode in the bar of the new Black Swan.

Two customers watch as their gins and tonics
keel over and tip their contents on the floor.

A full pint glass shatters into fragments,
and a tray of 20 glasses fires off simultaneously.

Heavily-sprung fire doors open and close.
Beer barrel taps in the cellar suddenly turn off.

Footsteps plod about upstairs.
And in the old Black Swan in the 1920s

a huge winged figure over the roof
doesn't like me just lying there in bed.

FREEDOM

For me to cross the road, mother holds my hand,
then leaves me in the market place.

I go to school alone, but when I'm back
I stand in front of Jimmy butcher's window

and shout 'Moother!' I'm ashamed. She hears me,
comes out, takes my hand, leads me across the road.

'Before I cross the road, look both ways:
first to the right, and then to the left.'

Rupert, my wire-haired fox terrier, can do it alone,
looks both ways though no one's taught him.

This Sunday morning, though, she's not looking,
and I don't look both ways, I just run

back and forth, back and forth, across the road
again and again in the way I'm not allowed to.

PERFORMING FOR GRANMA LOMAS

After neat thinly-sliced triangles of bread and butter,
brown and white, layered on a cake-plate,

tongue, tinned salmon, tinned pears and carnation milk,
home-made cake, jam and tea, with company,

she eggs me on to recite 'There are fairies at the bottom of
                                        my garden'.
It's a command performance, but I know her blue-grey eyes

are laughing at me, and I feel daft, but I do it.
Tucked away for her own exclusive use, she has

a whisky bottle in a cupboard: a little golden treasure
for special sipping. Dad pinches some,

puts water in and waits till she knows. Then he
roars with laughter and pulls out another bottle

with a flourish. Dad's the best-looking of the brothers,
the maddest, the most dangerous, and when he flirts with her,

she's a queen and he's a courtier, and she knights him
with her laughing crinkly-cornered grey-blue royal eyes.

For years and years my grandmother is in bed
with arthritis. She loves a joke and flirting with her sons.

Her bed's a sort of throne, and she's a queen
giving her grace to her daily rising son.

GRANDFATHER LOMAS

The master-dyer sits straight up,
legs slightly apart, never crossed,

a quiet twinkly watcher in a fireside chair.
Everything's straight, his bowler, or cloth cap,

the pipe in his mouth, which he takes out,
stem between first and second fingers, like a cigar.

He wears a waistcoat and a narrow white
stiff collar above a striped flannel shirt.

His moustache goes slightly down at each corner,
as he reads the paper with gold-rimmed glasses.

He's set it all going and paid for it, and now
he watches it all going its own way by itself.

He's calm, just waiting. All he has to do
is wait, and what's coming will come.

THE TOWN HALL

The Town Hall's more of a Money Box
than a Greek Temple. The Corinthian columns
are Greek but no means of support.

It looks difficult to get in. The Elgin marbles
in the architrave allegorise the goodness,
beauty and home truths of cotton, wool and industry.

And the Fielden Monument, finger in waistcoat,
celebrates the Ten Hour Act of 1847 –
cutting down the hours of toil for the kiddies.

Others should have stood in the bays
above the entrance – the pedestals are there –
but no one came.

A hundred years ago a crowd of
straddle-legged, akimbo men with
no women are standing by the lamp-posts.

The pile they've built is bigger but not bossier than they.
They're straight-legged, straight-eyed, straight-hat
what-about-it hands-in-pockets kind of men.

PRINCES AND TOADS

I watch the shine on Grandad's spectacles,
and his moustache. He lives in his fireside chair
in a household full of comedians and jokers.

He watches and smiles, dipped in his silence,
a master-dyer. He's trained only one of his sons,
my Uncle Jim, the eldest, in his trade.

There probably wouldn't be room for more.
My father's always got a sense of grievance
about his lack of a trade or an education.

He's had to make up his own life
with what he had after leaving school at twelve
and his brilliant mind and sense of comedy.

He notices everything, but he's reckless,
gets sad when he sees something beautiful
and he bows to no one.

He believes in truth, practises it
and makes me afraid to tell a lie.
He doesn't believe in God. There is no God,

and if there is He is no friend of his.
Perhaps it's the war but he did survive the war.
I think my Dad's unbeatable.

My Uncle Jim told my father
we were really Derby's. My father
behaves like a prince disinherited and disguised as a toad.

CORNETS AND TRUMPETS

In the first war my Dad was a stretcher-bearer –
in the Divisional Band. When the Battalion Bands
were broken up, they picked him out for the Division
above several bandmasters. Tested, he decided to play
his own improvisations on 'Rule Britannia'.
He got straight in. When the Battalion was stamping the square
he liked to kick a football about where they could see.

When armistice came he was offered a Trumpet
in the Hallé Orchestra, but he turned it down.
I'd a sweet tone, he said, *but I wanted
the musical background.* When I was fourteen
I longed for a Trumpet and got one through my Uncle Will.
We both used to play it – with the mute on –
till I slightly shifted a front tooth at rugby.

I'd learned to turn things down and once turned down
a fellowship. When my mother died my father
let the trumpet go with a pile of rubbish and my mother's
valuable clock: the lot for twenty pounds.
*You know, you could easily have mugged up any
music theory stuff you needed to know*, I said.
Aye – course I could, he said. *I know that now.*

Brass band music on the radio's hard to bear:
all those euphonious, sad, sweet, masculine sounds.

SOLDIERS

My Uncle Albert lied about his age,
joined up at sixteen, became a sergeant,

received a secret wound
and never had children.

Uncle Wilf was an infantry officer,
but didn't get picked off.

He still had his officer's pistol,
which weighed a ton when I played with Jack,

and the hammer would have
taken your thumb off.

My father was a stretcher-bearer.
Dad led the guffawing, the teasing,

leg-pulling his brothers and rivals
with lots to say and ways of saying it,

but though he met my Uncles Albert and Herbert,
by accident, near the Somme,

this was the only thing
they ever said about the war.

DAD

My Dad's a toff. He wears bespoke dark suits,
narrow stiff collars and sometimes knitted ties.

There's a clean white handkerchief
in his breast pocket, and his shoes

are shiny blackbirds. He tells me it's just as important
to polish the back as the front.

When he goes out with my mother he takes
a bowler out of a large wardrobe,

brushes it carefully with strong swipes
before covering his quiff.

He always looks people right in the eye
with king-of-the-beasts blue eyes,

knowing some joke they don't know,
smiling, but having them weighed up in a minute.

He'll have joined the mill at twelve, working
afternoons one week, mornings the next

at six-o'clock. In the back row at school
he'd feel sleepy, and the teacher'd kindly

let the half-timers sleep. At thirteen
he'll have gone full-time, ten hours a day.

Dad didn't learn much at school,
but he read Tolstoy, thought for himself,

and if he'd been a trumpeter in the Hallé
as he could have been, he mightn't have

married my mother, and I might still be
a ghost looking for a body to live in.

At night, other children wander above the clouds
wondering about the lives they never lived because of me.

ROCHDALE ROAD

Horsedung and snow on the Rochdale Road,
and the hens point their tails in the air
as they pick at the traffickless road.

The streetlamps are little taller than the folk
and modelled on giglamps
or lanterns on fluted columns.

We used to swing on the crossbar
for the lamplighter's ladder, and my dad was
once in love with the lamplighter's daughter.

White pots sit on the telegraph poles:
tall pines, wires and mind-forged
metal-contrived webs are sending along

news the boy doesn't know about
that will change his life. He walks
like someone going somewhere,

not just with two baskets to a shop.
Is it the feeling of coming from somewhere
that makes him lift his leg back so briskly?

And the other boy trotting down those
bulging cracked-pastry causeway-flags –
they have that walk from plodding the snow moors,

now cheek-cutting cold
with their starlings of dirt and white.
The houses are cosy.

They've comfy fires cut out of England
by bare-chested men
hacking and chopping long shifts.

The factory chimney's the pin
of a Catherine wheel, but so far there's still
fancifulness in the lamp-posts.

MR HYDE

He measures my growth regularly
with scratches on the wall.

When he plays cricket with us kids
it's as if he were playing for England.

Once he makes me laugh and giggle so much,
I say *Mother, don't talk to him!*

He's a lunatic! He goes red,
disappears in the bar, and I hear

the knock of a whisky glass on the mahogany.
Dr Jekyll's drinking his potion.

TRAM AND BERT

Dad was born weak and might die.
As a young man he was thin.

'Tram', short for Bertram, was a joke about 'tramlines'.
He built himself up with good butter.

Later he was 'Bert', a brawny name.
He admired Dr Johnson, thought of him

as an accomplice, though Johnson was ugly,
and my father was handsome.

But Johnson had a 'constitutional melancholy'
and spoke his mind. He hated cant, like Dad,

and, like my Dad, married a woman
ten years older than himself.

Dad tuned into the best music
with his uncouth longing for love,

searching for some obscure beauty in himself,
and healing his moods of self-contempt

with whisky and the companionship
of his fellow melancholic, Dr Johnson.

BRASS

The Lomas's are a cut above
everyone else, including the Garners.

My mother's Beatrice, but
the other Garners come from brass.

My Uncle Dick's bald head and shining
successful smile are made out of brass.

His Mason's status comes from brass.
True, the brass comes from his own brain,

but that's brass too and he glows with it.
He has big cars and a big house

with a tennis court and clock golf
but there's no brass without muck.

Unbeatable in big battles,
Lomas's need no Brasso.

REBUILDING

Men are pulling down the Old Black Swan.
Paradise is Going but Not Quite Lost.

We move to a poky little house
in Halifax Road, but there are new things,

new boys, and new girls, and
out in the streets at night new games.

We put on Fancy Dress Shows, turn
Uncle Remus into plays and act them out,

and in a long hot summer
we put on our swimming costumes,

and walk the hot pavements to Centre Vale Park,
and splash about in the Paddling Pool.

We get fat sunburn blisters, but
on the long walk home down Burnley Road

I feel naked. My body's out of place
among all this business and traffic.

THE ROCHDALE CANAL

Hillsides fold down from breast-top to treed slopes,
the cut of the canal, and the banks we used to walk
to the baths at Shade. We bought pies or parkin
with the bus fare, dawdling by dusty waters,
munching the gingery bread and fishing for frogspawn.
We came out of history too, redundant by the railway,
minutiae of the landscape, like a Roman road or an abbey –
we're glands and ducts of Dame Kind who remembers,
to walk along, look in, to fish in, or swim.

The Duke of Bridgewater, an Alberich licking the wounds
of unmasterable love, broke off his engagement
to cast out coal from his park at Worsley, where
Brindley accouched what Bridgewater conceived.
Aristocracy, art and economics engineered
generations of big-muscled bargees whose legs, clogging
the walls of quiet tunnels of stone-and-water echoes,
backs on barges, gently moved their watery homes
towards a sparkling exit, decorated with children and roses.

Eighteenth-century couplets of arches sent water bridges
gravitationally over Irwell on great viaducts,
deep into the Duke's earth, cutting the cost in half
of coal in Manchester. Big money, navvies
and stonemasons spaded, chiselled and styled
still more of the structures of childhood, the weeds
of the Rochdale Canal, the aboriginal railways
with grandiose branching lines, mills natural as trees,
and minds transmogrifying the earth with money.

Diving off the lock at Springside I pulled myself down
through bitty water to the mud at the bottom
and watched waving weed and brown sunlight

till water power pumped me up again into sparkling air.
A dytiscid beetle trapped in those waters
wolfed a half-moon steak out of the side of my stickleback
in the night, engraving me with quick-rowing legs,
digestive tracts, salivary glands and huge triangular
mandibles for competitive feeding.

FLY

We give our mice swimming races
in washing tubs, and I worry in case they're worried.

It's like the baths, so perhaps they like
paddling through the water, holding their whiskers up.

Once, though, I saw some boys pulling the wings off flies
and watching their funny walk.

I'm a mouse myself, looking back at me
out of the wet, and a fly waddling with no wings.

DARKNESS

The streets are dark, but with green gaslamps
and a bar to swing on.

And one night two girls show me what a girl's is like.
They squeeze the flesh round their elbow

into a little purse. It does look like that child's
hairless purse I saw one day by accident at the Paddling Pool.

It makes me go stiff. And bold. I pull mine out
and say 'That's what a boy's is like'.

They shriek with delight and run off down the dark street,
and I know that's what they wanted and I did it.

GULLIVER

Gulliver was tied to the ground with strings,
and little men were swarming all over him.

He pulled a whole fleet with his teeth.
Then he was sitting in the lap of a huge woman

with warty breasts. Giant women
teased themselves by putting him under their skirts

into their smelly private places, like I'd done
with my white mice when my Auntie Jane Anne

saw me and called me a dirty little boy.
The Houyhnhnms were clean and kept

the smelly yahoos in their place. In Laputa
the wise were stupid. They had to have a boy

to hit them with a bladder
and shake me out of my daydreams.

CHEMISTRY

I scoop the copper-sulphate blue, the yellow of the sulphur,
hypnotised by the test tube's shine,

the blue and orange of the bunsen burner,
the chemical changes of the colours, the magic rituals.

I'm an alchemist making gunpowder –
saltpetre, sulphur, and iron filings.

I create bonfires in little tin-tops.
Put the powder in a corked test tube, heat it

and it'd make a big bang, and I want to.
But my steam engine's controlled power,

and it works, with its brass boiler,
inlet for water, and a safety valve on a spring.

The chimney's only for show, because
the boiler's heated with blue spirits.

I pour in the spirits, light the wick and wait.
The water begins to boil, and a pipe leads steam

down a piston like the pistons on train-wheels.
The piston moves, and it whirls a wheel round,

which drives machines I've made with my Meccano.
They start to revolve, and I'm alone with all this power.

I pour some blue burning spirit on the linoleum
of my bedroom, and it goes on burning there.

I watch it, and it doesn't set the house on fire!
I do it again and again, and it makes my dick go stiff.

SCIENCE

I've got *The Wonder Book of Science* for Christmas,
and there's a brilliant oval spectrum on the cover,

and inside photographs of artificial lightning-flashes,
though no one knows what electricity is.

At grammar school we're asked. *Who knows
what science is?* I say, *Yes, I know:*

it's seeing how nature works. Then we do
nothing for a year but convert inches into centimetres

and back again. Science's been shown up:
just a boring way of making us do arithmetic.

And after that I'm no good at science, but
the teacher's eyebrows go straight across his nose

in a thick black bar, and when he talks he has to
keep licking his lips like a dog eating.

It's much more interesting than science.

LIFEBOAT DAY

There's something about a Lifeboat.
Todmorden's about as far away as you can get
from the sea in the British Isles, yet
the first Lifeboat Demonstration in 1895
commands not only a Boat towed through the land
but Officials, the Fire Brigade, and six bands.

After Fireworks at Home Fields,
cheers, high jinks and a Town Hall Concert at eight
the town will sponsor it every five years.

The procession's watched by belles and swells.
You can see how serious it is
from the men's and ladies' hats
and the way the men grip their lapels.

MAD MOUSE

One of my mice gave birth to babies:
tiny pink hairless creatures, like baby pigs.

I wanted to show them off, and anyone interested
had a peep in the smelly box.

There they were: mother and family
exposed to the light, and big faces

staring down at them. Girls got very excited.
Boys wanted to handle them.

The mother ate her little ones, went mad,
gnawed her way out of the wooden box

and escaped into the walls of the house.
Later, when my mother went mad

for a while, I remembered the mouse.

KEITH

Lying awake, we were both
a bit too excited to sleep,

and he said *Do you ever get stiff?
How do you mean?* I said

*You know, between your legs.
Your dick.* Yes, I think so, I said.

*Does it make you stiff
just talking about it.* Mm, I said.

His hand went slowly onto my dick
and found that it was stiff.

I could hardly breathe.
But then I put my hand onto his,

and of course it was stiff. *Do you ever
get a funny feeling?* he asked.

Mm, I said. Soon we were both
rubbing each other and having funny feelings.

His mother was divorced, a teacher,
and had asked me to sleep with him.

She thought, I suppose, I'd be
a kind of brother for her only son

and a good influence.

RABBIT

He keeps the rabbit I'm buying
in a remote attic. It's a large white animal,
the size of a hare, perhaps it is a hare,

with a powerful kick and a bad temper.
Put your hand in the hutch,
and the beast'll go for it and bite.

You slide its pot of food carefully
inside its hutch. When we're up there
the boy wants to suck my dick.

In spite of shame I let him,
and it gives me such a very powerful funny feeling
I have to ask him to stop.

Afterwards I'm scared, and ever after
the buck rabbit is guilt. I keep him in a hutch
nailed in the coal shed at the height of my head,

and his unnatural violence is a punishment
for my unnatural behaviour. One day,
when mother's feeding him,

he falls out of the hutch and
breaks his leg while I'm at school.
When I'm back from school

the accident and the execution are over.
The dead rabbit's been fed to Long Bob,
who sweeps up at the pub, is poor

and has a big family. They say it was delicious.
Long Bob and his family always seem
unnatural to me, like cannibals.

KISS

I kiss a girl in the dark coalshed
where I keep the rabbit.
I've never been so close to breath,

I hardly dare touch girls, and this
is more than touching,
this is tasting and smelling

and feeling a whole girl's body
next to mine. Then she tells me
how children are made,

and I'm unbelieving and burning
and believing
and somehow I don't hear her.

DOBROYD CASTLE

Turreted on the corners and with a tall keep
it's a full-size version of my toy fort
without the drawbridge. It's stood there for ever –
a place to climb to, natural as a nettle, unquestionable.

The men who imagined it wore hats like
mill-chimneys and rode light carriages.
Their intangible fantasies turned into mills
and castles and a whole county.

Swankier and more show-off than the stars,
it's the Fielden mind, castellated, battlemented,
neat nineteenth-century stone masonry,
each stone like a brick, with curved corners on sash windows.

Toil for the unemployed is a tax on the rich.
Hired men hew a waymark of surveillance,
making the surveyors surveyable.
Look down and eyes look up. A castle's like

wearing a diamond the size of a boulder.

DRINK

   1.
My Dad stands with Dr Bailey,
holding his arms out at shoulder height.

Dr Bailey likes a drink himself.
Both Dad and Dr Bailey are joking

about the shaking. Dad is over
the hallucinations now,

not drinking, so becoming nice again.

   2.
The young Town Clerk from Cambridge,
Mr Simmons, comes to our hotel

as a boarder. My mother admires him, so handsome,
courteous, and well-educated, a gentleman.

He seems to like and quite admire
my Dad, and one day they're off to the races

and have 'a drink or two'. Next morning
I hear Mr Simmons retching in the lavatory.

Poor Mr Simmons… Is he
Dr Jekyll becoming Mr Hyde?

   3.
One day my Dad's showing off by
running across a builder's plank

that sways up and down, bouncy,
going to a third storey window high above the yard,

and he falls. He keeps straight and lands on his feet,
breaks his ankle and his heels

and always has a slight limp after that.
He flourishes a knobbly ash walking stick

and makes his limp a swagger.
In a pub one day, when he's eighty,

a young man takes the stick outside,
and breaks it in two. He must have seen

something in my Dad that scares him.

LOVE

   1.
She likes to sing and play
a particular song. It's her song.

> *Gone are the days*
> *That to me were so dear,*
> *Long, long ago,*
> *Long, long ago…*

One day she's suddenly gone
and never comes back. I ask why.

Mother takes me on her knee
and says, *One night*

when I'd gone to bed before your father,
I woke up and realised he wasn't there.

I went downstairs and there he was
with this girl on his knee.

I feel old and don't know what to say or do.

   2.
I've set up my tent on the grassy patch
above our back yard. This girl

is a maid at David Greenwood's,
whose father runs a shop called The Emporium.

She's sitting inside my tent,
a queen in the glow of the canvas.

She points to some little dry spots
on her lips and says, *Do you know what those are?*

No, I say honestly. *Kisses*, she says,
smiling in a satisfied way.

BILLY HOLT

Billy Holt was put in prison in the Town Hall
for shouting communism in the market place.

At the mill, learning German,
he wrote the words in dust on his loom.

He travelled the world with a horse
and slept beside it and wrote books.

It's rather odd, he wrote, *that I,
a working man, should admire*

*true aristocracy. Some there are,
born natural aristocrats,*

*and can be recognised at once.
It has nothing to do with money.*

*When an aristocrat gets up to go out
the common people open doors for him.*

FATHERS, SONS AND DAUGHTERS

In very old age at last, and longing for death,
my Dad, with just the evidence of the big body

and gritty will, remembered me roly-polying
and how fast I did it in Todmorden park –

and he made me choke at the two of us young,
he thirty, running faster than me.

Once he could hardly run fast enough
to stop me roly-polying into a lake.

Pear trees in the wind, blossoms
confettiing off in the spring,

pears bumping the ground in autumn:
air in the tree, wind oxygenating off

the Pennines, or drenched from the Atlantic,
prevailing, knocking off pears and people.

If science could do it would you
resuscitate every human being who ever lived?

And somewhere I'm always climbing down a cliff
with a girl on my shoulders. The sun's

a blinder, and neither will ever grow old.
Picnic in hand, a bottle in the other,

we climb down to the sand. But where's the sea?
That must be it – a glint over there.

And later, hours later, we find the crack in the sea
the sun goes into and go back.

And somewhere I'm always
climbing the cliff with the girl on my shoulders.

The sands are behind. The hotel's gone.
The island's growing no older. The food's

for ever as good and always remembered,
the happiness, the wine, the big dinners, the talk.

WHERE ARE YOU NOW?

As I lie in bed, I hear you
playing and singing downstairs.

Pale hands I loved beside the Shalimar,
where are you now, where a-are you now?

You have the customers singing,
solo or together *Nelly Dean*,

In the Shade of the Old Apple Tree,
Down at the old Bull and Bush.

When I wander through the smoky
'back room' in the evening, given beery cuddles,

you play *Darling I am growing o-old,*
Silver threads among the gold,

specially to bring tears to my eyes,
relishing your power to make me weep.

Grey Days are your grey eyes,
Grey skies your hair…

And, after all, you were singing to yourself,
in your early forties, and still are,

and, hopelessly, grey skies and days still are
that dark hair of yours and your grey-blue eyes.

ROOMFIELD SCHOOL

The school builders must have
thought of it as a Chapel, without a spire,

Gothic but crouching. It's a stone lid
over the soil to culture this flat place

where we go through the Market
and down the narrow lane by the Calder

to the Infants' Class and are worried
by the smells of urinous trousers and individual bodies

and the hands raised to leave the room.
On the sills are the jam jars of sticky buds

and tadpoles, and at the break
there's the sickly milk or the Horlicks.

We sprain our brains with arithmetic and spelling
and if we're good Mrs Graham will read us

The Wind in the Willows.
When she goes out of the class

the little girls stand up and show us their knickers,
and we write our reports on the books we've read: 'I liked it.'

This is the slot we're posted through,
more or less carefully, and come out

the other end a different letter.
This is the millstone grit school

with the unmarried ladies in their beards
and long noses in *loco parentis*.

On the corrugations of the playground,
where the rusty-headed policeman's son

twice our size bumped his chest against ours
and twisted our arm, were we really,

like good poets, learning to erect
aspiring cathedrals out of our weakness?

Why do we need so much weight against us
to construct Charles Atlas muscles

or tumble to our weakness and give way?
Why, to slip through the slot of night,

must we be humped in a postbag all the day?

URINE

My first day at school girls
put up their hands up and say
Please may I leave the room.

They're openly admitting
they have wee-wee-outs
and want to wee-wee.

One boy sits in yellow corduroy
short trousers, always smelling of
wee. He does it in his trousers.

He sits in his urinal smell,
withdrawn and guilty,
a dog in disgrace.

I still remember the hot wee
flowing in my sleep
and the wee-wee shame.

BOOKS AT SCHOOL

I've already learned to read
from Rupert's balloons,

but here we learn to read and write
with our tongues.

We say capital 'A's and small 'a's
aloud together as a class.

Our Miss points to the letters
on the blackboard with a long stick.

Then, twisting our tongues,
we copy them between the two blue parallel lines.

We stand up in turn and read aloud from books
that show girls in old-fashioned frocks,

and we learn poetry by heart: *The fairy
nidding nodding in the garden,*

and *Old Mother Cherry blowing her nose.*
I'm huddled in the wigwam with Old Nokomis,

and up in the sky Gitchegoomi watches over
me and Minnehaha, Laughing Water.

The Indian corn grows from a grave,
and I know that death's not death

as I sail off in my canoe on my long
last journey into the sunset.

OUR HEADMISTRESS

Our headmistress stands at morning prayers
like a general. She's on parade.

She wears a dress of flowered cotton
down to her ankles: it's her uniform.

A fold rises crosswise across her chest
from her waist to her neck.

Then it becomes a sort of dog-collar
surrounding and hiding her neck.

My Dad says she tried to cut her throat,
and the collar hides a scar.

My eyes linger under her yellow face
on the collar. What is there underneath?

ALL THE ANIMALS OF EMPIRE

Britannia used to appear on every penny.
She seems to have gone, taking her
helmet and trident with her.

When Lord John Sanger came to town, with a carnival
of humping elephants, snarling tigers, white-horsed
equestrians, clowns and a military band,

nine horses hauled her coach. She was the top perch
of a quadruple-decker steam organ, carved with
staring Charons, bowed old men, scrolls

and field-marshal-faced red-and-gold
lions with bristly moustaches. A top-hatted coachman
gripped a clutch of reins,

backed by brass-helmeted soldier boys with pikes and shields.
Top peak of all, Britannia, in nurse's uniform and brass hat
sailed past the rooftops, a perilous girl.

The young men argued in emulous admiration
of her bonzer world-whacking beauty, till they got a close-up,
and the shock of her masculine sergeant-major face.

KNICKERS

In the top infant class,
as soon as she's out of the room,

some girl stands up, lifts
her skirt and shows her knickers.

If she's gone long, one boy,
sometimes two, will pull their

dicks out and show them, long and stiff.
Lenny has a surprisingly large one,

which curves slightly like a banana.
It makes him seem weird.

Is there ever an eye watching
through the little glass cabinet in the wall?

TEACHERS

Those with nice faces, like Auntie Madge,
marry and have to leave teaching.

Mrs Graham sometimes comes
when teachers are sick,

and if we're good she reads us *The Wind in the Willows*,
but she's not the wife of Kenneth Graham.

She has black eyebrows and black eyes
like the stern commander of a sinking ship.

Bertha Longnose is greasy-skinned
and straggly-haired. Why does she have a nickname?

The other teachers are all 'Miss'.
Even my Auntie Madge knows her nickname

and smiles at it, which I feel is somehow wrong.
I don't remember any poetry

or exciting extras in her class, but once,
when I've taken a test and finished early,

she twinkles at me kindly, and she
almost seems beautiful, as if

an angel has come and stood over me.

AQUARIUMS

Our classroom has high windows,
so we can't see out, with blind,
ribbed glazing on the lower panes.

On the spring windowsills there are
jamjars with sticky-budded twigs
and sticklebacks in glass tanks.

In our aquarium we watch
caterpillars making little coffins on a leaf.
Then they come out wet and spindly-legged,

not the plump soft bags they've been.
I net frogspawn in the canal
and the little black spots in the jelly

turn oval, grow heads and eyes,
wriggle tails like blades,
push out legs, lose their tails

and finally turn tiny, squat,
throbbing frogs in striped skins.
I float in the water with them,

glassy-eyed, like on rainy Sundays,
when I sit among the Victorian furniture
and stare at the large window, where flies

crawl up the window, buzz
down again and toil up again,
as the raindrops hit the glass,

bulge and spill down the pane,
while the flies buzz dreamily
or fizz despairingly.

OLGA

Olga Wadsworth sits in a window desk,
with sunlight haloing her golden hair.

She's almost transparent, with eyes
like rainy bluebells in the wood.

I put my hand down to the bottom
of their cold squeaky white stems

and break them off just above
the bulb, dripping with raindrops.

But you could never touch
Olga Wadsworth, or even speak.

She's not a body, or even a flower.
She comes to my birthday party, but

all the glitter of cake and sparkle of lemonade
fade like the other children in her gold.

I don't speak. It's enough she's in the room.
She opens her eyes at my prince's kiss.

Then her family goes to America, and
I never see her again, except in films.

I see her in 'Our Gang', just for a moment,
and then she disappears behind another child.

MARJORIE GREEN

We know why we're going up
the hillside past Kenneth Marshall.

He's playing football in white shorts.
He smiles in a funny way,

as if he knows, and we climb up
among the trees and get under the mac.

We're both shy, and I can see her face
twitching like a deer.

We're just being close, very close,
touching and smelling each other,

feeling each other a bit, and it's
lovely hugging under the mac,

but afterwards we pass
Kenneth Marshall again

and he looks very healthy,
and next Saturday I'm there,

playing very hard, sliding about
a lot in the mud and coming back black.

MARY PRIESTLEY

Walking to school and back
across the market place
and down Roomfield Lane

I stare at the River Calder
through the iron gate in the stone wall.
Coming back at four

I climb the high black wall
in the playground, put my toes
in the footholds between the stones.

I'm climbing a mountain rock-face
to the higher street where Mary
lives in her house, and I might

get a glimpse of her
and she might stare and look away.
When I'm eight, in Bertha Longnose's class,

I'm moved up to Miss Lord's,
who has a beard. Everyone's older than me,
and they all know long division and fractions,

and Miss Lord, with her black beard
and red face, doesn't like me,
and soon I go deaf.

But Mary Priestley is there.
She passes a little folded note
from desk to desk,

whispering *Pass it on*,
and it says *I love you*.
At playtime I run up to the iron gate

like an aeroplane and hurl
my bomb across the bars:
I love you.

She picks it up and runs off with it,
and all the other girls shriek.
I wander the streets near her home

after dark, hoping she'll be there.
and we can play together,
hot with curiosity, never touching.

We'll swing on the green horizontal bars
on the gaslamps, play marbles
or skim cigarette cards,

but often she's not there.
The girls are constantly hopping,
skipping and jumping,

with ropes, crossing arms, dancing on one foot.
I roller skate everywhere,
swooping down the steep streets,

heading for each lamp post
and swinging round it
to check the rush.

THE RECHABITE CONCERT PARTY

    1.
I'm in a charabanc with a lot of
chattering smelly girls.

When we're there they powder
and perfume their bodies

with nothing on but knickers and vests
and then dance bare-legged on a chapel stage.

They link their arms, do high kicks
and dance in line like real chorus girls,

stamping the stage with their dancing shoes
to put the stress on the words:

> *Tinkle, tinkle, tinkle,*
> *What if the stars don't twinkle.*
> *Tie a little bell to your dancing shoes*
> *And the stars will shine.*

They begin to sweat, and then they change,
and I can smell them, and I try not to stare.

I'm shy and I'm the only boy,
but the girls aren't shy. They like me looking.

    2.
Dressed in my diplomat's uniform,
cocked hat, white stockings,

knee-breeches and eighteenth-century
tailed coat with gold tracery,

I march to centre stage, bow and speak:
The chorus will now perform "The Stars Will Shine".

I bow again and walk away with dignity.
When my own turn comes I announce:

*The next item is a recitation:
"The Knight" by Geoffrey Chaucer.*

I walk off and walk back on. I know
it's rather daft, but it gets a chuckle.

   3.
I always have stage fright.
Even the charabanc's sickening.

The Rechabites are a temperance society.
Someone on the platform says

landladies are loose women.
I've heard bad things about

'publicans and sinners' in church too,
but my mother explains that 'publicans'

in the Bible are really tax-collectors.
Once, on the way back, the respectable

white-haired Rechabite in charge,
obviously fond of me, sits me on his knee.

I know this isn't quite right somehow
and sit very stiff. Is anything what it seems?

SIN

Mary Priestley's in the chorus.
She's older than me.

I don't speak to her, but we look
and we both know and remember:

that day in our big bathroom
at the end of the creaking lobby.

One day when we were about two
we were all looking at each others' bottoms.

Kenneth Marshall was prizing the cheeks
of some girl's bottom slightly apart,

to see better, when my mother came in.
Though she was little she looked big

in the bathroom door and she bundled everybody out.
She wouldn't speak to me all day.

She whisked her skirts disgustedly away
as I tried to clutch at them in the kitchen,

and Mary Priestley had left
a black and guilty turd in a little tin potty.

STOODLEY PIKE

The portico of Stoodley Pike's the entrance
to a tomb of gold-masked kings, but who's

buried there, except perhaps the wind?
The big oblong hole of huge black stones

was built by flying lizards. No light-slits
lighten the stairwell. You spiral up the dark

to the big balcony and the stone balustrade
built to hold you back, an audience for the moors.

As you stand there, your stomach's flying down
the swerve of the opposite hillside, and your gob's

stopped by the strangling wind. Where are you going?
You're emptier than the black stairwell,

or the winds on the tops that stop you speaking.

LISTENING

The wind's listening, and the rain on Whirlaw,
and the valley's long shadows in the evening.

A late blackbird breaks in on the quiet
of moss and lichen, and I know I'm here.

The trees know I'm here, and someone else
knows I'm here, listening, as I'm listening.

It seems like myself, only older, stranger,
knowing I'm not really the little boy I am.

RUPERT

Rupert and I roam Whirlaw and Stoodley Pike
together, happy in high wind or heavy rain.

This is the life: he runs four times farther than I,
back and forth, happy in the freedom and friendship.

One day there are pools of what looks like spit.
Then on the hillside Rupert seems to be having trouble

breathing. He lies down tired. Then he coughs up
one of these pools of spit. I press gently on his chest

to help him breathe, but a cloud crosses his eyes,
and I know he's looking at death. We go slowly back,

and that week mother takes Rupert to Rochdale,
and he never comes back, and I know not to ask why.

DOG SHOW

I entered him for the dog event
at the Cattle Show in Centre Vale Park,

but after he'd been bathed
he rubbed himself back and forth

along a whitewashed wall
and was muckier than ever.

Moreover, he refused a lead.
He'd never had one.

A neighbour, though, lent me
his fox terrier, 'Crackers',

a well-groomed slave dog,
with a better beard,

and his back legs
thrusting out at the proper angle.

The ponce won the first prize,
and there I stood in *The Todmorden Advertiser*

in a smart suit and a Jimmy Coogan cap
with a clean dog that wasn't mine on a lead.

ALBION BARKER

Albion Barker, the organist, though small,
is enormous behind me.

He sends my back waves of hatred,
and he must hate 'The Harmonious Blacksmith'

even more than I do. All I want
is to play like my mother.

But as I sit here, seeing my fingers
mirrored in his grand piano's black shine,

so different from our own brown
upright fortepiano that plays 'Nelly Dean'

on beer-stained strings, I know my
real fingers are in the wrong place.

GRAMOPHONE

Under the mahogany lid
there's a smell of rubbed metal and static.

The baize turntable, the shiny
fold-back head and the tiny

tin box of bright needles
with a treble clef on the lid

make a boy sing 'O for the Wings
of a Dove' and 'Hear my Prayer'

from the black disc with
the whirling dog in the middle.

How nice, my mother sighs,
if you could sing like that.

And the next day I've asked to be
a 'probationer' in Christ Church choir

though I'm only six
because I'm that sort of boy.

CHRIST CHURCH

Christ Church stands with black pricked ears
and clocks among the dripping trees.

I take the back lane down the worn stone steps
between the church and the sooty black trees.

The church has blackening angels in its graveyard.
The vicarage is where the murders were.

But inside there are gold-speared wrought-iron gates,
a gold cross parked on the choirstalls,

lights, a reredos and music. I walk into an orchestra
of violins, trumpets, flutes and bassoons,

and out of a scratchy old record of
'Hear My Prayer' and 'Angels Ever Bright and Fair'.

THE CHOIRMASTER

Mr Dennitt's fingers are white vermin,
with a life of their own, crawling the keyboard
of the groaning harmonium.

Their cold flesh and bloodless whiteness
come from the cuffs of a dark bank-clerk's suit.
He sways a little, backwards and forwards,

his ear cocked to you, and his eyes
like bats behind his large horn-rimmed glasses:
watching you even when they aren't.

He has ears and eyes all over his body
and in the back of his head.
He has Harold Lloyd's glasses,

though you'd never see him
hanging from a clock
in a crowded street.

His eyes belong to his bony white crabs that
creep up the scale, and he's an exalted being from an organ loft,
come down to our little vestry in disguise,

and it's weird, it's somehow wrong
when I watch those same fingers counting banknotes
across the shiny mahogany countertop of Lloyds' Bank.

CHOIRBOYS

Smelly behind their stiff white Eton collars,
black bow ties and starched surplices,

their hair's like marram grass.
I always noticed the whiff of one boy,

and the sweaty beads on his forehead.
He's dark, almost black, with shiny eyes,

and his brother says he sweats so much
because he's always fucking girls.

Smithy and I walk up the hillside
from the vestry to a cave,

to smoke woodbines or cinnamon bars,
and Smithy tells me 'fucking' is what

some dirty lads do: they put their dicks
inside girls' holes. That's how babies get bom.

And did our mothers really
let our dads do what that lad does?

SEEING STARS

They claim I scratch my head by
putting my arm over the top of it
and scratching behind the other ear.

There's a lad with a little perky nose,
oriental eyes and banana-shaped lips,
like a girl's. He's popular, a sort of mascot.

So one Sunday when they're all
getting at me, I go for him. He's my size,
and I'm hitting out at the lot of them,

and they know it, egging him on,
when his fist hits my eye, and I see
an astonishing star: amazing.

It's a flash I thought were only pointy shapes in cartoons.

FUNERAL MARCH

We stand by the black soil
as the box goes down on straps,

and we sing: *Yea, though I walk through
the valley of the shadow of death...*

So death's a place to go to. Back
in the choir stalls the organ booms and beats,

and Nick goes stiff, stands to attention
and breathes *The Dead March!*

The Dead rise. Invisible footsteps
tramp silently round the aisles

to the organ's hullabaloo. Nobody warned me
the dead were coming here too!

RIDGE-FOOT HOUSE

The dignified gate and driveway through the leafy garden
past the greenhouse to this moneyed stone house by the Mill
whose chimney fell when the Great War broke out

becomes a big white Olympia with marble floors
from Italy. Now faces of Frankenstein and Dracula
dream-play science, technology and capitalism,

while, behind all this, I kick my shoes
along the stone-kicking road to Christ Church
where the indissoluble ménage

of economics, suffering, necessity and force
was never christened, nor their divorce.

LEAVING THE CHOIR

The only words I can ever remember
him saying to me alone was when I said I was leaving.

He looked at me gravely. *I was leaving
just as I was beginning to be useful.*

It was a big surprise. I thought I'd been useful all along,
I didn't know I was only on a path to usefulness.

SLUMP

There's no one in the bar.
The taproom's deserted. The cards,
the piano, the dominoes are still.

Poverty hovers over the rooftops,
pours down with the rain, drenches
the roads and the streetlamps.

Depression seeps between the pavement stones,
dampens the bedclothes, sits on the windowsills,
watching the neighbours workless and waiting.

Dad's giving beer away to old customers.
That can't last long, but it's more cheerful,
and Dad's playing jovial with them.

Are we poor? I ask mother, seeing
a paleness on her face I know is poverty.
Poverty's an illness. Its symptoms are

worry and men in cloth caps sitting on cobblestones
outside the walls of closed-down mills,
and it may be catching and worse.

THE GOLDEN LION

In the photo the Fielden Memorial stands with
head cocked, waiting to welcome

the first-ever double-decker bus.
It comes rattling over the cobbles in mid-road,

fearing no on-coming traffic, with a bouquet of
bowler-hatted, wobbling joyriders on top

and an admiring procession trapesing
and gallivanting behind.

A single lonely man plods round-shouldered,
cobble-watching, past the Golden Lion,

with his back to it all. All this prosperity's
doom to the financially depressed.

DEPRESSION

I sleep in a top-floor bedroom
at the end of a long uncarpeted corridor
of creaking boards and empty rooms.

No one else but me sleeps or lives up here,
except an invisible black-winged bat
that hovers over the roof.

I lie in bed and look out onto
wastes of supernatural space
where malignant spirits materialise at will.

They prefer to be invisible,
but they hang about outside my bedroom door
and peer through the wallpaper

and watch from the black window.
I'm too scared even to take my
clothes off. I feel safer in clothes.

I get in bed with them on. Dare I put
the light out? It's scary, but I'm brave
and then I lie doggo in the inhabited dark.

In the photo my face is pale, overtired,
with dark rings round the eyes,
knowing the black-winged bat behind me

filling the pavements with the unemployed.

THE SENTENCE

Our sentence is exile from the Black Swan.
It's final, and there's no appeal.

I'm living in a story with a rotten plot.
It's too big for me, and I don't know how it'll end.

The foxes have holes, we have no home,
but it must be our fault.

I live with Auntie Edith, just
a short walk across the 'Rec' to grammar school.

My father and mother come occasionally,
visitors, both putting a brave face on.

They're a penniless, rather handsome couple
who live at my grandad's.

But now I see very little of them,
and when I do they're people

I once thought would be there for ever
who are just passing through.

AUNTIE EDITH

She bakes wonderful cakes and lets me
scrape out and eat the sweet raw dough
from the sides of the mixing dishes.

The house is fragrant with the prospect of
dark brown bread or light lemony flavours,
spongy textures, or slab nut-and-fruit slices.

Sometimes I can eat them while they're warm.
The whole house smells good and wholesome.
She's beautiful, even though

the skin on her face has an angry chapped
reddishness, caused by frostbite in Canada,
where my Uncle Herbert once tried his luck.

She stands and walks as though she's
showing visitors into the drawing room
of her stately home. I stare at the inlay in the chairs.

Her beauty shows in her wallpaper
and the little tables with delicately-shaped
china ornaments, whose intricate designs

carry important indecipherable messages.

UNCLE HERBERT REXSTREW

I know the word 'Rex' from pennies,
and his name makes me think of a king.

He's a man of tall distinction, thin,
with thinning hair and thoughtful eyes,

but now he's always in his chair,
his pulse beats visibly in his neck.

He's a clever. He knows about books and politics,
can think and talk, though lacking schooling.

He listens carefully to what I say,
and once he applauds a remark I make

and asks my Auntie Edith to listen to it.
I'm pleased but feel shy, as if on stage.

TOMMY DODD THE DAISHER

This was the nickname given to Philip Ridgeway of Watty Hole ('daisher' being the local dialect for 'dashing young man')... Philip Ridgeway was postillion for Bill Barrett who rode out in a carriage drawn by twenty-four goats, Tommy Dodd running alongside. He also visited farms in the neighbourhood for the purpose of killing pigs for the farmers and was noted for the fact that all the pigs he killed appeared to have thrived without needing livers as part of their anatomies.
   – Roger Birch, A Way of Life, Glimpses of Todmorden Past, 1972

Even the dog's got an unswerving back
and a miss-nothing, metal-glint high IQ look,
his tail up between his legs like an erection.

Tommy Dodd's and the dog's lips
have the same despotic downcurve, though
the dog's are humourless and incapable of irony.

Dodd's a ramrod. Whatever policy his liver
and the livers are proposing, his vertebrae
prop him up like a tentpole.

His head has the horizontal slightly ruddled
policeman's eye-gaze of a
disproportionate carnival mask.

Left hand on glass, the other's been
thumping the arm-rest to hammer a point
about how people ought to go about things nowadays.

The dandy double-breasted waistcoat with double buttons,
huge flapped pockets, broad buttoned-down lapels
and a shackle of a watch-chain dangling like a security measure

has stood firm against the midriff and many winds.
The trousers would drop to the floor with their own weight
and no doubt he often did it with his boots on.

Behind, the photographer's screen's been prinked out
with some effeminate flowers,
a Matisse-like pillar and a balustrade.

It contrasts with the serviceable tablecloth
and Tommy's serviceable hard jaw. The hard words
from that mouth and the know-all regard from
                                      the heavy-lidded eyes

will be the last word and eye-opinion on every topic,
biffed out with the manner of wit if not wit itself,
which there well might be in those days of creative talk.

There are no doubts in Tommy's mind on livers
or the cure for love. Out of the props Todmorden provided,
and a twenty-four goat carriage, a big waistcoat

and liverless pigs for slaughter,
he put together
a photographer's screen of a face.

GOODBYE TO THE VALE

As a child I was told 'Todmorden' meant
'The Valley of the Fox'. Later I learned
'Tod' was was German for 'Death'
and 'Morden' Swedish for 'Murder'.

Later still I read that 'Todmorden'
means 'Totta's Boundary Valley':
property names the animals
and all the boundaries.

Hlumhalghs – Anglo-Saxon for
'Lomas': it means 'The Well
in the Little Narrow Cleft',
a lost place somewhere in the North.

A Lomas lived at Blackshaw Hall,
the Vale of Todmorden, in the twelve hundreds,
and we were driven out of the Vale
in the depression of '35.

The night before we left I watched
fireworks burst and scamper
for the Jubilee of George V:
the inauguration of our end that started here.

WRITER'S WORKSHOP AT LUMB BANK

Not only a childhood but a century's infancy
is gone through a black hole in the galaxy.

These crumbling mills are the rubble of
clogged generations dispersed in the night.

The cotton-mill-man who built this house
and fixed the polite table where the poets

now sit with typewriters had nothing like this
in mind. Would he understand these words

and new well-soaped genetic arrangements
he's somehow given rise to? Child labour's

retreated to another part of the planet.
Oliver Twist sits in the clean lady's ideal home,

but not at the end of the novel, in the middle.
Life deals out its new unknowns, and its

trump of unpredictability. We sit here,
at other work, in our penultimate orphanage.

CROSS STONE CHURCH

When mothers die and they bury them
on snowy mountainsides in black and white
    Pennine mornings, after cold service
      in millstone grit unheated churches

sons will often bide at gravesides
feeling the ligaments of flesh –
    the other end of the cord
    now underground,

tense as a worm pulled from the earth,
tugged and tugging back in a beak,
    taught the quiet roadway
    under the hill with the cars.

But sons, so tugged by ghosts and
guests, must move to the banquet,
    guests of honour, but guests,
    past flowers to the cars.

It never ends: on ventilated summer days
coasting the sun-patched moors in cars
    their mothers bought
    with money left,

driving the hills with well-loved wives,
they'll know they're taking the same roads
    down the intersecting valleys
    with the telegraph poles,

beneath Black Stone Hill
where they used to walk with their dogs.

HAWORTH

From Liverpool we could return to a strange country
for half-a-crown: three busrides, two changes
and we were up the steep Haworth street to a private winter:
invisible weekends in the Bronte Guest House
with *The New Statesman* in the breakfast room and
arctic sheets after nightwalks in the graveyard.

In the Black Bull bar we sat by the fire where
Branwell drank himself into opium,
though we were outside on our minds, hair flying,
Cathy and Heathcliff, windshouldering the tops
in the landscape of Emily's head,
with the gale in our throats and eyes.

This was where they watched each other
spit blood and imagine. Looking into her great
cat's eyes, I watched my astonished exit
into greater uncertainty. We watched each other
as lovers and our way of loving and into our loving
we dredged our own and these other lives.

'ARTEMIDORUS FAREWELL'

> *The mummy case of Artemidorus; a young man of about twenty-one; with a painted portrait; from Hawara; Roman period; second century A.D; the British Museum.*

Artemidorus, you were loved by the goddess,
called early by the one who sends plagues and death
among men and animals. Did she then
cure and alleviate you, as Isis perhaps,
on those lion altars of the other world,
protectress of the young? But Artemis
is a maiden deity, never conquered by love,
unlike your family, who bought you
such a beautiful coffin, preserving
the personality in your face till now.
She slew Orion with her arrows because
he'd made an attempt on her chastity.
She changed Actaeon into a stag simply
because he'd seen her bathing.
She slew the children of Niobe
who deemed herself superior to Leto.
She's represented as in love with
the fair youth Endymion, whom she kissed
in his sleep; but this legend properly relates
to Selene as the Moon; it's foreign to
the character of Artemis, who was,
as we observed, unmoved by love.
As a huntress her breast is covered
and the legs up to her knees are naked,
the rest being covered with the chlamys.
As the goddess of the moon a veil
covers her head.

       I'm looking at the red and the
black and gold of your beautiful mummy case
and thinking of the bundle inside, and a cold bit of earth
on a Pennine hillside, where two old people
were buried in winter and still haven't a stone.

HERBERT LOMAS, poet, translator and critic, was born in the Pennines, served with the infantry 1943-1946 ,including two years with the Royal Garhawal Rifles on the North West Frontier of India, and graduated with first-class honours and an MA from Liverpool University.

His *Letters in the Dark* was an *Observer* book of the year, and he has received Guinness, Arvon and Cholmondely awards. His *Contemporary Finnish Poetry* won the Poetry Society's 1991 biennial translation award, he is a member of the Finnish Academy, and he was made Knight First Class, Order of the White Rose of Finland, 'for his services to Finnish Literature'. Of his nine books of poetry only *A Useless Passion* is still in print.

A former Senior Lecturer at the University of Helsinki and Principal Lecturer at the University of London, he lives in Aldeburgh, Suffolk.